GOD'S WONDERFUL
WORLD

JAN GODFREY AND PETER ADDERLEY

Once upon a time, a very long time ago, there was nothing, nothing at all—except God, the great and wonderful God.

"I am God, and I will make light," said God, "clear, pure light. Let there be light!"

And there was bright, beautiful, dazzling light, as clear and brilliant as transparent glass.

God, the great and wonderful God, looked in wonder at the bright and beautiful light, and he was pleased with what he had made.

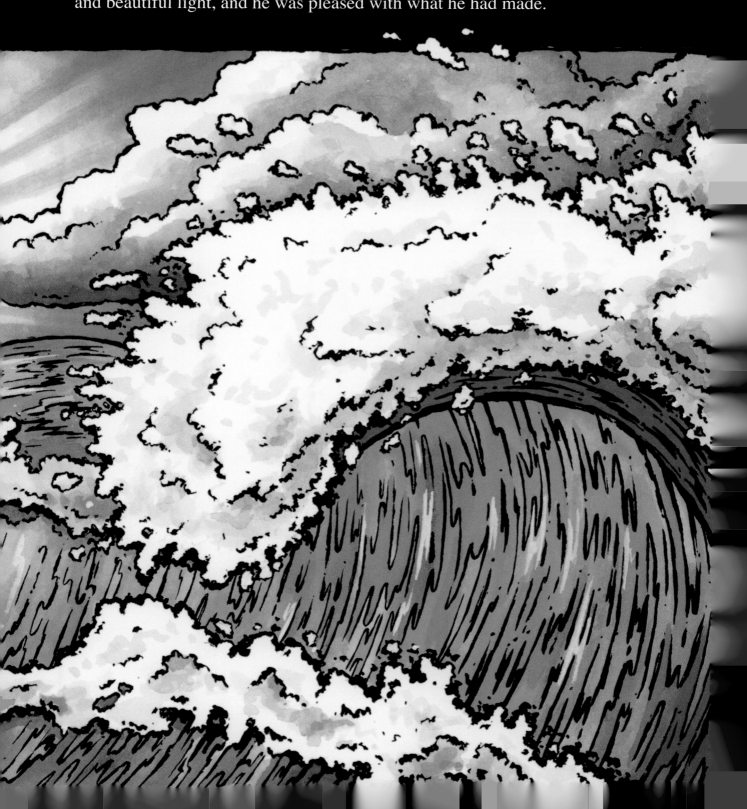

"I am God, and I will make land and sea," said God. "I will make dry land and wet sea, volcanoes and mountains. Let there be land and sea!" And there were! God made firm, solid land; high, cold mountains, pointy and purple; and hot, rich, fiery volcanoes.

Then there were great, deep rolling seas with blue, green, and gray splashing waves. God, the great and wonderful God, looked at the earth, the sky, the sea, the mountains, and the volcanoes, and he was pleased with what he had made.

"**I** am God, and I will make plants and trees," said God. "I will make tiny plants and great spreading tree trunks. Let there be plants and trees!" And there were! There were soft, green mosses and thorny, prickly plants. There were big trees and little trees, spreading leaves and tangled

creepers, scented shrubs, fruity bushes, and feathery grasses.

God, the great and wonderful God, looked carefully at the patterns in the mosses and the tree trunks and leaves, at the bushes and the shrubs, and he was pleased with what he had made.

"**I** am God, and I will make flowers and fruit," said God. "I will make delicate flowers and good things to eat. Let there be flowers and fruit!"

And there were! There were cheery sunflowers and tiny daisies. There were round oranges and bunchy bananas. There were opulent orchids and hairy coconuts. There were colors and scents and knobbly, squishy, juicy, peely things.

God, the great and wonderful God, looked happily at the colored flowers and fruits, all different shapes and sizes, and he was pleased with what he had made.

"I am God, and I will make sun, moon, and stars," said God. "I will make heavenly lights to shine in the sky. Let there be sun and moon and stars!" And there were! There was a golden, flaming daytime sun. There was a shining, silver nighttime moon.

There were millions of twinkling, glittering, faraway stars.

    God, the great and wonderful God, looked in wonder at the great rolling, burning lights, and he was pleased with what he had made.

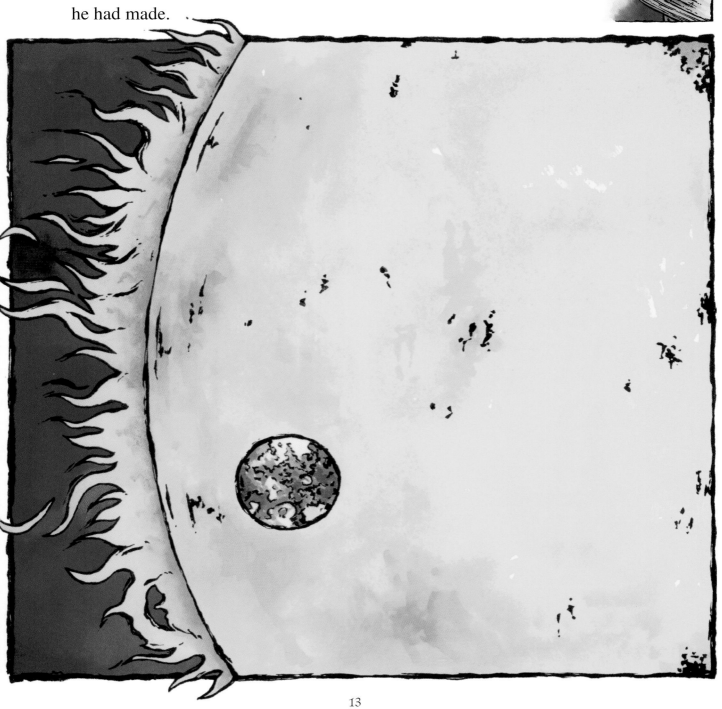

"*I* am God, and I will make fishes and sea creatures," said God. "I will make fishes great and small. Let there be fishes and sea creatures!"

And there were! There were great whales and sharks that churned through the sea. There were quick little colored fishes that darted and dived, flipped and flapped and floundered in the waves.

God, the great and wonderful God, stared into the blue sea, and he was pleased with what he had made.

14

And God made creatures on the sea bed, strange and curious creatures that lived deep, deep down in the waters.

There were seahorses and shells and water snails. There were squirmy worms and squiggly squids. There were octopuses with eight

wiggly arms, seaweedy rocks that looked like creatures, and creatures that looked like seaweedy rocks.

God, the great and wonderful God, looked down to the deepest sandy depths, and he was pleased with what he had made.

"I am God, and I will make birds with wings," said God. "They will walk about in the rivers, dig in the mud, and fly through the air. Let there be birds!" said God.

And there were! There were flamingos and pelicans and puffins, emus and ostriches and toucans. There were swans and geese and ducks that walked and waddled all over the land and waded in the water.

God, the great and wonderful God, smiled as he watched the birds dipping and dabbling and caring for their young, and he was pleased with what he had made.

*A*nd God made birds that sang and soared and swooped high in the sky, and he made other flying creatures, too.

The birds flew up and down to their nests and in and out of the trees. They flew over the mountain tops and across the great wide sea.

The butterflies, bees and bats, insects and moths flew and fluttered and buzzed. God, the great and wonderful God, looked in delight as their wings moved the air and their sounds filled his world, and he was pleased with what he had made.

"I am God, and I will make more animals," said God. "I will make large, noisy animals that stamp and stomp, trample and tread, and run and roar and jump for joy. I will make small animals that hop and scamper and squeak—and slithery, slippery snakes. Let there be all sorts of animals!" said God.

And there were! There were zebras and moles, ladybugs and lemurs, and tapirs with long, wobbly noses. There were hoppy frogs and toads, geckos and gazelles.

God, the great and wonderful God, laughed with his noisy animals, and he was pleased with what he had made.

God gave some of the animals patterns and others prickles.
He gave some long ears and others long noses. To some he gave
swishing tails and to others wiggly horns and pointed tusks.

There were patterned giraffes, patchy pandas, and tigers with stripes.
There were long-eared donkeys and slothful sloths. There were prickly

porcupines, smiling alligators, and crafty crocodiles. There were wild, mischievous monkeys and stamping, trampling, trumpeting elephants.

God, the great and wonderful God, loved the variety of shapes and patterns, sizes, colors, and sounds, and he was pleased with everything that he had made.

"*I* am God, and I will make people," said God. "I will make man, and I will make woman."

And God did! He made people who would be his friends, people who would live in and enjoy and care for his world, the great and wonderful world that he had made.

27

"I am God, who has made all the people in the world," said God. "I have made men and women and children to love my world, to look after my world, to care for all the plants and creatures, animals and fish and birds, and everything else on the earth, and in the sky, and in the sea."

Then God looked very lovingly at his world and all the people in it.

"Look after it for me," said God quietly. He had finished making the world, his wonderful world, his colorful creation—our wonderful world, our wonderful God. "Take care of it."

Library of Congress Cataloging-in-Publication Data

Godfrey, Jan.
  God's wonderful world / Jan Godfrey and Peter Adderley. — 1st
North American ed.
    p. cm.
  ISBN 0-8198-8317-4
  1. Creation—Juvenile literature. I. Adderley, Peter. II. Title.
  BS651.G751 2008
  231.7'65—dc22

                                    2007029914

Edition copyright © 2008, Anno Domini Publishing,
1 Churchgates, The Wilderness, Berkhamsted,
Herts, HP4 2UB, England

Text copyright © 2008, Jan Godfrey

Illustrations copyright © 1997, Peter Adderley

First North American edition 2008

Published by Pauline Books & Media,
50 Saint Pauls Avenue, Boston, MA 02130-3491.
www.pauline.org.

Printed in Singapore.

Pauline Books & Media is the publishing house of the Daugh-
ters of St. Paul, an international congregation of women
religious serving the Church with the communications media

1 2 3 4 5 6 7 8 9   11 10 09 08